BEARING WITNESS

GENOCIDE AND ETHNIC CLEANSING™

ETHNIC CLEANSING IN THE
SYRIAN CIVIL WAR

BRIDEY HEING

Rosen
YA

NEW YORK

Published in 2018 by The Rosen Publishing Group, Inc.
29 East 21st Street, New York, NY 10010

First Edition

Library of Congress Cataloging-in-Publication Data

Names: Heing, Bridey, author.
Title: Ethnic cleansing in the Syrian civil war / Bridey Heing.
Description: New York : Rosen Publishing, 2018. | Series: Bearing witness : genocide and ethnic cleansing | Audience: Grades 7–12. | Includes bibliographical references and index.
Identifiers: LCCN 2017011106 | ISBN 9781508177340 (library bound) | ISBN 9781508178668 (paperback)
Subjects: LCSH: Syria—History—Civil War, 2011– | Syria—Ethnic relations. | Genocide—Syria. | Ethnic conflict—Syria. | Syria—History—Civil War, 2011-—Refugees.
Classification: LCC DS98.6 .H45 2018 | DDC 956.9104/231—dc23
LC record available at https://lccn.loc.gov/2017011106

Manufactured in China

On the cover: The Free Syrian Army, backed by Turkish government forces, accompany civilians after securing the Turkey-Syria border against Islamist extremists.

CONTENTS

INTRODUCTION

Throughout modern history, there have been a number of humanitarian crises. Among the most horrific are cases of ethnic cleansing, or the targeted killing or removal of a specific group. Examples of ethnic cleansing include the Holocaust and the Rwandan genocide. Both were carried out during the twentieth century. In the twenty-first century, it became clear that ethnic cleansing occurred in Syria, where a civil war broke out in 2011.

This map of Syria shows Iraq, Lebanon, and Turkey, some of the countries bordering it. The capital city, Damascus, is also marked.

It's no coincidence that popular protests swept through the Middle East and North Africa during the same year that Syria's civil war began. These protests, called the Arab Spring, challenged several long-standing authoritarian governments in countries like Libya, Egypt, and Bahrain. But in Syria, a country located in the very heart of the Middle East, protests were met with the full force of the government, and that conflict escalated into a civil war.

The civil war has meant crisis for the civilians of Syria. Fighting between rebel groups and the government of Bashar al-Assad has displaced millions and left thousands dead. Instability has also made the country a safe haven for extremist terrorist organizations, including the Islamic State of Iraq and Syria, or ISIS. And many international observers have shared concerns that there are particularly sinister elements that combatants have contributed to the conflict. Syria used to be a fairly diverse country because it was home to many religious and ethnic groups who lived somewhat peacefully together, but during the conflict, divisions and tensions between these groups have become flash points for fighting. Rebel groups, the government, and terrorist organizations have been accused of carrying out genocide against specific groups.

Fighting has made it difficult for observing international organizations to gather verifiable information about possible war crimes committed during the conflict, but the United Nations and others have presented evidence that multiple groups, including the government, rebels, and ISIS are targeting civilians, instead of opposing armed forces. Civilians were attacked with chemical weapons, bombing, and execution. There is a wide range of reasons for this violence, including the Assad government's willingness to attack civilian areas under rebel control, and ISIS's desire to show their strength and control territory. But while the reasons for the violence are tied closely to the civil war, the tensions that led up to the violence existed before the civil war began.

Tracing the roots of this conflict can help people to understand it. How the Syrian Civil War began, the ethnic and religious groups that call Syria home, and how those groups have come under threat since fighting began can offer insight into how a meaningful end might be brought to this conflict. And learning about how the international community has responded to the conflict and what readers can do to help those suffering in Syria will put the conflict into perspective to an uninvolved observer.

CHAPTER 1

SYRIA BEFORE THE WAR

In order to understand how fighting developed between the factions that have become engaged in this war, we have to understand the history of Syria since the early twentieth century, when the Ottoman Empire collapsed and France and Britain took control of the Middle East. It was during the period of British and French rule that the boundaries of modern Middle Eastern states, including Syria, were drawn. But those borders were drawn with too little concern for ethnic divisions within the newly formed countries.

SYRIAN INDEPENDENCE

Syria was once home to numerous ancient kingdoms and empires. The country is home to cities, including Aleppo and the capital, Damascus, that are among the oldest in human history. It has a rich history, including creating trade and government and facilitating the coexistence of diverse ethnic and religious groups.

In the seventh century, Damascus became the temporary capital of the new caliphate, or Islamic Empire. The Ottomans conquered the area in 1516, making it part of the empire that controlled most of the Middle East until after World War I. After their loss in World War I, the Ottoman Empire (including the Ottoman Caliphate) was divided between France and Britain under the Sykes-Picot Agreement of 1916, which established the borders of modern states in the Middle East.

Syria fell under the French mandate. Unrest was common under French rule, with rebel groups challenging French control of the country as early as 1920 in attempts to establish their own government. However, Syria would remain firmly under French control until 1936, when protests managed to convince the French to negotiate a treaty of independence.

This photo shows Aleppo just before the civil war began. It has been an important city in the area now known as Syria since ancient times.

However, France never ratified that treaty, so another decade of conflicts between the Syrians and the French culminated in France giving in to pressure from the international community and from Syrians to leave. The last French troops withdrew from Syria on April 17, 1946.

THE ROLE OF COLONIAL RULE

France governed Syria with a series of local administrations that divided Syria into six states, one of which would become Lebanon. The states were based largely on sectarian divisions in the country, and included Damascus, Aleppo, Jabal al-Druze, Alawites, and Sanjak of Alexandretta. All of these were governed independently and overseen by a high commissioner.

The French hoped that keeping ethnic and religious groups separated would allow them to rule longer, but all factions were opposed to French rule. When it became clear that the local population would revolt against them, the French began using ethnic and religious divisions to maintain control. This was a common tactic in colonial states, where occupying powers could encourage groups to fight one another rather than unite against the occupying forces. By isolating ethnic and religious minorities, France also created a sense of unity among those communities rather than a national Syrian identity that could have helped overcome divisions as they moved into self-rule after independence. The British promoted similar dynamics in Africa, and the ethnic tensions those colonial forces encouraged set the stage for genocide to take place in countries including Rwanda.

This photo depicts Hafez al-Assad, the man who took advantage of the instability in Syria to make himself the president in 1970.

Unrest did not stop when the country became independent. For the first decades after achieving independence, Syria experienced a number of coups. In 1949 alone, two coups overthrew multiple governments over the course of the year. That unrest would continue in Syria until 1970, when the defense minister, Hafez al-Assad, took control of the country in a coup.

DEMOGRAPHICS AND TENSION IN SYRIA

Even if colonizing forces saw them as such, Syrians and those in other Middle Eastern nations were much more than just a ruled people. Thus, to understand the powers at play during this era in Syrian history, it is important to know the ethnic and religious makeup of the country.

When fighting began in 2011, Syria's population was around twenty-two million people, with Arabs making up about 90 percent of the country's ethnic makeup. Kurds made up the majority of the remaining 10 percent, while Armenians made up around 2 percent.

Most Syrians are Muslims. The majority of the country's citizens are Sunni Muslims, but the Alawites, a Shia offshoot, have ruled the country since 1970. Sunni Muslims, who follow the more widespread iteration of Islam, account for about 74 percent of Syria's population, while the Shia Muslims and Alawites make up just 13 percent. Alawites are known to be secretive about their beliefs in part because of their small numbers, but they consider themselves a branch of Shia Islam that draws inspiration from Judaism and Christianity as well.

Alawites of the Ba'ath Party march to defend their position of power after the Assad regime installed them as the dominant power.

Sectarianism in the government was a source of conflict even before the civil war, as non-Alawites alleged that the Assad government had favored Alawites for positions of power.

There is also a small Christian minority in Syria, including Assyrians who identify as descendants of the former Assyrian Empire (located in portions of modern-day Iran, Iraq, Syria, and Turkey). They have been persecuted by Islamic extremists after the civil war began and so they often side with the government.

In addition to sectarian influence, ethnic tensions were rising before the conflict of the civil war. Syria is also home to Kurds and Yazidis. Kurds are an ethnic minority that practices various regional religions, including Islam and Christianity. Kurds live in several regional states, but they are the largest ethnic, stateless minority in the world and have long called for an independent Kurdistan centered near the Syrian-Iraqi-Iranian-Turkish border. Countries in the region, particularly Turkey, have regularly refused to acknowledge Kurdistan as an independent or completely separate sovereign entity. In fact, some have even engaged in violent skirmishes with militant Kurds. There were around 1.8 million Kurds in Syria as of 2011 (slightly less than 10 percent of the population) and 30 million worldwide.

Yazidis are a religious minority and are ethnically Kurdish. Their religion is a monotheistic one with elements of ancient Iranian religion, as well as Judaism, Nestorian Christianity, and Islam.

The Druze also have a small presence in Syria. They make up about 3 percent of the population. The Druze are an ethnic and religious group that does not allow conversion, and their small numbers mean that the group is largely isolated. Their numbers seemed even smaller in 2011 because they were more spread out throughout Syria. Like Alawites, their faith is believed to blend Christianity and Islam.

THE ASSAD GOVERNMENT

Hafez al-Assad established a one-party state in Syria under the Syrian Ba'ath Party when he came to power in 1970. Under

Assad, the country became an authoritarian state, with Assad tightly holding all power. He put Alawites, a religious minority, in charge of the military and intelligence community. This act of dominating the Sunni majority underlined sectarian differences between the two groups.

Assad also introduced pragmatic economic policy, making Syria a stable regional state aligned with Arab interests. He strongly opposed Israel and the United States and formed strong alliances with the Soviet Union and Iran. Assad ruled Syria until 2000, when he passed away.

By the 2000s, Syria became stable and had a per capita gross domestic product (GDP) of about $5,000, close to the average for regional states. Education was widespread for both men and women, with literacy rates at between 80 percent and 90 percent across the country. But these stabilizing elements were a limited part of the environment that the next ruler of Syria would inherit.

Bashar al-Assad took part in an election in 2000 that saw him win the presidency, but the election was conducted with an unopposed ballot; Assad was the only candidate. Although early on in his presidency Assad was seen as a possible reformer, he quickly began cracking down on dissidents and protests. Security forces commonly detained people (some of whom were political prisoners) without arrest warrants and engaged in torture, and economic inequality left the majority of Syrians struggling for opportunity even as elites became wealthier.

Under the Assad family, power has been held primarily by Alawites, although since the civil war began the central government controlled little of the country. As of March 2017, Assad was the leader of both the Syrian Regional Branch of the Ba'ath Party and the National Progressive Front, a socialist coalition of parties that supports Assad's rule through controlling the legislative People's Council of Syria.

Prior to 2011, in spite of its prosperity, Syria faced serious problems. Concerns about corruption and inequality were widespread, and the government had little regard for human rights. Then, a drought between 2006 and 2010 strained the economy and removed an important stabilizing element. This drought forced many of the country's most vulnerable people into poverty by causing already limited resources to become scarcer. The drought also caused farmers to move into cities in search of work. These changes laid the foundation for the unrest that would eventually spark widespread protests.

CHAPTER 2

HOW THE WAR BEGAN

The Syrian Civil War began in 2011 with protests. At the time, it wasn't clear how Assad's government would respond to large-scale demonstrations. In fact, the government initially promised reforms that were meant to satisfy protesters, although they were clearly contrary to the government that Assad's father led. Not delivering on those promises caused the situation to deteriorate from marches in cities to a full-on civil war.

THE ARAB SPRING

On December 17, 2010, a young fruit vendor named Mohamed Bouazizi self-immolated in front of government buildings in the Tunisian city of Sidi Bouzid. He later died of his injuries. He had been frequently harassed and targeted by police forces, and this made it difficult for him to support his family. His suicide was a desperate act of protest against Tunisia's government, and it sparked massive demonstrations across the country calling for the resignation of Ben Ali, the country's authoritarian president. On January 14, 2011, twenty-three years into the president's reign and just twenty-eight days after Bouazizi's shocking act, Ben Ali fled to Saudi Arabia and resigned. His resignation cleared the way for Tunisia to begin transitioning into a democratic government.

This November 15, 2011, photo shows the family of Mohamed Bouazizi, the fruit vendor who self-immolated to protest Tunisian authorities that had been harassing him.

This successful protest, known as the Jasmine Revolution, set off protests across the Arab world denouncing high unemployment, income inequality, corruption, and human rights violations. From North Africa to the Gulf Emirates, authoritarian regimes were challenged by large marches and protests in major cities. Within a few months of the resignation of Ben Ali, the Mubarak government was overthrown in Egypt and the Muammar Gaddafi regime was overthrown in Libya, with other states seemingly close to regime change as well. These protests became known as the Arab Spring, and they signified the people overcoming repressive governments.

In Syria, protests began in the city of Daraa in March 2011. They were in response to the alleged torture of high school students who were caught writing graffiti on a school. Several protesters were killed when security forces opened fire on them, and this incident sparked large protests around the country. Crowds gathered across Syria to call for democratic reform, the end of emergency law, and greater freedom. Their tone would change in April, when demonstrators began calling for Assad's resignation.

Security forces began moving against protesters that same month. The earliest days of the war were characterized by sieges in cities like Daraa, where the protests began, and Homs and Baniyas. These sieges were an attempt to subdue growing dissent, but they only led to more protest around the country, including in Damascus where mass arrests were carried out. By the end of May, around one thousand civilians had died in clashes that arose between protesters and Assad's regime.

GOVERNMENT AND REBEL FORCES

In July 2011, the civil war began to take shape. Former officers in the Syrian armed forces formed the Free Syrian Army (FSA), one of the primary rebel groups fighting the Assad regime. The group carried out guerrilla attacks against military targets around the country, sometimes with little coordination between fighters and the group's leadership. Although their tactics were sometimes disorganized and they were significantly disadvantaged when it came to weapons, the FSA was able to take control of northern and southwestern parts of the country by late 2011.

Fighters with the Free Syrian Army are shown here after they secured control over Tel Tuveyran and Kaarat villages of Al Bab town.

In August 2011, the Syrian National Council was founded. It was made up of multiple anti-Assad groups that served as an exiled force that worked to represent the interests of Syrians and arm the rebels, and their coalition was based in Turkey. Assad began using the military later that year, and by 2012 rebel groups were fighting with Syrian forces as both sought to claim territory. As the fighting evolved, Sunnis largely sided with the rebels while religious and ethnic minorities tended to side with the government.

Kurdish fighters, who were aligned with the rebels against Assad and with the Syrian National Council, were on the forefront of fighting ISIS. This caused tension with Turkey and called into question whether the Kurds will seek an independent state in the civil war's aftermath.

FOREIGN FIGHTERS

Nonaligned groups and foreign fighters quickly joined the fighting in the Syrian Civil War. Al-Nusra Front, also known as Jabhat al-Nusra when it was founded, is one of those groups. It was founded in Syria in August 2011 by Abu Mohammed al-Julani, who came from the Islamic State in Iraq (ISI), and whose purpose was to create another offshoot of al-Qaeda. In fact, ISI's leader, Abu Bakr al-Baghdadi, and al-Qaeda worked in conjunction to enable al-Julani's activities.

In 2013, al-Baghdadi announced that al-Nusra Front was joining forces with ISI and that this new, consolidated group would be called the Islamic State in Iraq and Syria, or ISIS.

Al-Nusra Front leadership announced that no such merger was taking place, and this caused al-Nusra Front to split into two main groups: one that changed its name to Jabhat Fateh al-Sham (still known as al-Nusra Front) and remained loyal to al-Qaeda proper and one that joined forces with ISIS. There were also those who simply broke away from ISIS and al-Qaeda by leaving the group.

A foreign group that would come to hold more territory than al-Nusra Front is ISIS. ISIS's territory includes parts of northern Syria. ISIS follows an interpretation of Sunni jihadist extremist Islam that emphasizes the importance of its own strict guidelines. Anyone who falls outside of a very particular ideal, or who does not follow Sunni Islam, is considered to be *kafir*, or an "unbeliever." According to ISIS teachings, carrying out acts

Members of Islamist extremist group al-Nusra Front carry a banner depicting Jerusalem's Dome of the Rock and a slogan in Arabic.

of violence or sexual assault against people who are kafir is not a crime. This is the logic that excuses the ruthless violence that ISIS has inflicted upon Yazidis, Kurds, Christians, and Muslims who do not support them.

More than a dozen extremist groups that are not aligned with ISIS or al-Qaeda also exist, including Sham Legion and Ahrar al-Sham. Most of the militias and armed groups in Syria are Sunni extremists, fighting against the Assad regime but not on behalf of the rebels. The number of combatant groups that experts know have a presence in Syria is staggering, with estimates of about one thousand or more.

A HUMANITARIAN CRISIS

Organizations like the United Nations have struggled to verify reports of human rights abuses. We do know, however, that civilians are being tortured, killed, and starved by government forces and rebel groups alike. There are reports that ISIS uses fear and terror to control populations under their control, with public executions and sexual assault used as common tactics. In 2016, UNICEF estimated that around one in three Syrian children have known only war, with around 8.4 million children impacted by the fighting and around 6 million needing humanitarian assistance. Millions are unable to attend school, and many do not have reliable access to clean water, food, or medical care.

PEACE TALKS

Peace talks have occurred since 2011, when the Arab League started them in November. The earliest talks were able to secure the government's agreement on a peace plan, but a group of observers sent to Syria in December of that year were quickly recalled from the country as violence escalated. In 2012, Russia became more active in peace talks, and the United Nations Security Council began debating potential frameworks for ending the violence. No agreement was reached at that point, however, in part because the United States, France, and Britain believed that the Assad government would fall in a matter of months.

Kofi Annan, the UN's envoy to Syria, addresses an audience in Geneva on June 30, 2012.

In June 2012, the United Nations envoy to Syria, Kofi Annan, began a conference in Geneva. The United States, China, Russia, and Great Britain took part in the talks, which resulted in an agreement that a transitional government including members of the Assad regime and the opposition should be established. Later that year, a ceasefire was brokered by Algerian diplomat Lakhdar Brahimi between the Syrian government and the opposition to coincide with the Muslim holiday of Eid al-Adha. But both sides accused the other of violating the agreement, and fighting continued.

Despite numerous ceasefire agreements, no end to the war has been brought about as of June 2017. There are many reasons for this, including a lack of agreement on whether Assad should be allowed to stay in power. But one of the most complex issues around the conflict is that foreign groups and fighters are often not included in ceasefires. Many of the concerns that made the earliest negotiations fail still loom over the conflict.

CHAPTER 3

THE CONFLICT RAGES

The protests that resulted in the civil war continued into 2012, with thousands taking to the streets in cities across Syria. Defections from the Syrian government continued, and suicide attacks and bombings on government forces took place with greater frequency. The state began cracking down harder on protesters, bombarding cities under siege in order to retake them from rebel factions. Between 2012 and 2014, the scale of violence increased significantly and included events like the rebel forces successfully seizing eastern Aleppo from government control in 2012. This is the period in which ethnic cleansing became a defining characteristic of the conflict.

THE INTERNATIONAL COMMUNITY RESPONDS

Estimates from the United Nations state that by February 2012, the death toll had risen to more than 7,500. In the wake of such widespread violence, the United Nations Security Council and the General Assembly voted on proposals related to Syria during the same month to try to resolve the conflict. In the General Assembly, a statement condemning the abuses taking place in Syria was passed, along with a call for Assad to step down. In the Security Council, an Arab League proposal that would have called for Assad to step down as president did not pass because Russia and China vetoed it. In July of that year, the Security Council voted along the same lines on a resolution that would have placed international sanctions on the Syrian government.

By March 2012, countries had begun shutting down their embassies in Damascus. In April 2012, countries began formally recognizing and supporting the Syrian National Council, an Istanbul-based group in exile that is seen as representing those opposed to Assad. That month, the United States pledged to support the group logistically and later in the year announced $45 million worth of nonweaponry aid, while Arab states opposed to Assad pledged around $100 million in aid.

COMBATANTS FROM FOREIGN GOVERNMENTS

The governments of foreign countries have been involved in the fighting in Syria since the earliest days of the conflict. Iran is one of Syria's closest allies, so that country's military helped to train Syrian army and government forces. Russia had been accused of aiding Syria with air strikes against rebels, and the powerful and influential Lebanese Shiite group Hezbollah sided with the Assad regime. Iraq is also believed to have sided with the Assad regime, in part because the country allowed Iranian planes and supply convoys to travel through Iraqi airspace and territory.

Hezbollah militants traveled from Lebanon to Syria to support the government forces. Hezbollah forces are one of many groups active in the Syrian Civil War.

A coalition of nine countries, including Canada and the United Kingdom, have conducted air strikes against ISIS targets in Syria. Additionally, thousands of fighters from around the world have traveled to Syria to join groups like ISIS. The United States and Turkey have taken the lead in supporting the rebels, although the United States' support for Kurdish fighters in Syria is something Turkey does not agree with.

Turkey has been at the forefront of supporting the anti-Assad forces since the early days of the conflict, and in 2012 tensions between Turkey and Syria increased when a Turkish jet was shot down in Syrian airspace. Although the two countries did not formally go to war, Turkey announced that it would engage with any Syrian troops near the border who were interpreted to be a threat.

ETHNIC CLEANSING RESHAPES SYRIA

The landscape of ethnic cleansing in Syria tells the story of various assaults on different groups and how that has reshaped the geographic breakdown of the country. Before the conflict, the Druze were primarily located in Jabal al-Druze, in southwest Syria, and Idlib, in northwest Syria, while Alawites were primarily in the northwest. Kurds and Turkmen were clustered in the north and northeast, and Christians and Alawites were in the west.

The Syrian government, rebels, and extremist groups have all been aligned around a strong sense of ethnic or religious identity, so in several instances they have resorted to attacking groups they perceived as different or threatening to them. As a result of fear and the violence that had already transpired, people in particular ethnic groups, including Bedouins and Turkmen, and religious groups, like the Shia and Druze, flocked to certain areas to preserve their safety. The territory that ISIS came to

On November 25, 2015, refugees flee air strikes that the Russian and Syrian government conducted on the Turkmen town of Bayirbucak in the Lattakia region of Syria.

control became the most homogeneously Sunni Muslim, due in part to Christians, Shia, and other religious minorities fleeing. This separation also represents ethnic cleansing: minorities were forced out of certain areas and into others that would be more homogeneous.

Militias that support the Assad government have also carried out war crimes against civilians, in part out of fear that the fall of the Assad regime could mean their own extermination. While ethnic groups fleeing from aggressive militants is one type of ethnic cleansing, the act of one group attempting to kill all in the opposition (as opposed to simply trying to gain control over them), or all who simply are different in a particular way, is another type.

By March 2013, the conflict had created more than one million refugees, and in the next month, extremist Islamist groups began taking more territory and implementing their own efforts to purge the areas of minorities that did not align with them.

THE ATROCITIES OF ISIS

In April 2013, the Islamic State emerged as an influential force in Syria. ISIS's goal was to create their own state, or caliphate, which they had hoped to govern using a violent and extremist interpretation of Sunni Islam. They wanted to control territory. That is why the group was in conflict with both rebel groups and Assad's forces.

Within the area ISIS came to rule, they have used terrorism against the population to control them and have made violence a political tool. But on top of that, ISIS uses mass extermination for ideological reasons.

Much of the known violence carried out by ISIS has taken place in Iraq, where Iraqi forces reclaimed territory. In Iraq, we know that ISIS has carried out mass extermination, torture, and sexual enslavement against Yazidis, Christians, and Shia Muslims. In one of the group's best-documented cases of ethnic cleansing, approximately fifty thousand Yazidis were forced onto Mount Sinjar in Iraq in 2014. ISIS planned to let them stay there so they would starve to death. At the same time, ISIS fighters killed thousands of Yazidi men in nearby villages and towns, while taking women as slaves. Iraqi Kurds were able to break through into Syria to create a safe passage into Iraq for those on the mountain who were confident in their ability to survive the journey. They, along with Syrian Kurds, were able to push ISIS out of Sinjar, but the Yazidis have little confidence in the longevity of their safety in Iraq.

Less is known about ISIS's violence in Syria, where international organizations have struggled to gather accurate data, and civilians have had a harder time fleeing. Individuals found smuggling information or video out of ISIS territory, including the de facto capital, Raqqa, are executed in public. What has been learned about life under ISIS is that it is ruled by fear and punctuated by public displays of violence meant to present the leadership as all powerful. Laws favor ISIS supporters and make anyone who does not follow the group vulnerable to abuse, exploitation, or execution. The fact that ISIS kills anyone perceived to be working against them or not following their leadership constitutes a form of ethnic cleansing that aspires to make a once-diverse city homogeneous in religious belief and practice.

However, it is clear that the Kurds have been on the forefront of the fight against ISIS and have effectively carved out a ministate for their population near the Turkish border. Their growing role in the fight against ISIS and their support from the United States and other Western powers could lead to conflict between the Kurds and the governments of Turkey and Syria when the civil war ends, forcing governments to decide between recognizing a new state or setting up a potential further conflict in the area.

This Kurdish Syrian Democratic Forces soldier, as well as others from the
autonomous region of Rojava, Syria, has helped regain territory that the

WAR CRIMES

War crimes, including ethnic cleansing, are established by international law. Although norms for war have existed for centuries and governed acceptable behavior during combat,

ISIS IN THE MIDDLE EAST AND AFRICA

ISIS has become associated largely with Iraq and Syria, where the group is most active and was first established in 2013. But ISIS is active across the Middle East. They carry out attacks against non-Sunni Muslims and those who do not follow the group.

Across the Middle East, ISIS has also worked to undermine governments by carrying out bombings, suicide attacks, and other planned violent activities to create chaos. In both the Middle East and Africa, where ISIS is less active, the group has created a network of extremist groups that are loyal to ISIS leadership and to some extent take cues from the group's core leaders.

Ethnic cleansing has been most visible in Iraq and Syria, but it is part of ISIS's ideology and could be carried out by the group anywhere they have significant power. ISIS has stated their goal is ridding Sunni Muslim culture of all outside influence, which means creating a society in which their distorted interpretation of Islam is the only recognized religion and cultural source. Isolating themselves would require eliminating all ethnic and religious diversity in any given area. They have done this with some success in parts of Iraq and Syria. ISIS's goals can only be achieved through ethnic cleansing, making them dangerous to all individuals and cultures.

it wasn't until the 1949 Geneva Convention that international treaties bound the international community to a set of laws regarding treatment of people in a war zone.

Ethnic cleansing is a war crime, but it is only one of many that have allegedly taken place during the Syrian Civil War. In late 2013, a United Nations-led fact-finding mission determined that there was substantial evidence that the Assad government was responsible for war crimes against civilians, including mass killings carried out between 2012 and mid-2013. According to the report's findings, these killings played a role in the large-scale displacement (approximately 4.25 million people) that took place in Syria.

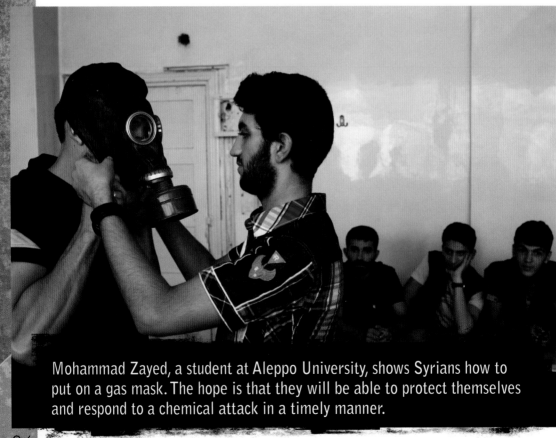

Mohammad Zayed, a student at Aleppo University, shows Syrians how to put on a gas mask. The hope is that they will be able to protect themselves and respond to a chemical attack in a timely manner.

The use of gas and chemical weapons began around May 2013, with a sarin gas attack that rebels carried out against the government. In June 2013, the United States alleges that the Syrian government used chemical weapons against civilians. This claim gave justification to providing military aid to rebel groups. Assad has allegedly carried out more chemical weapons attacks against civilians, including an attack in August 2013 in a Damascus suburb, in September 2014 in areas around the country, and in April 2017 in Idlib Province. In May 2014, Human Rights Watch issued a report alleging that the Syrian government had used chlorine gas on civilians in rebel-held areas.

STALEMATE SETS IN

The continuous violence of the Syrian Civil War has driven millions to flee fighting, but also led to little change in the circumstances on the ground. According to Max Fisher at the *New York Times*, this is simply because no one side is strong enough to win: "Because neither Mr. Assad nor the rebels are strong enough to win, the battle lines push back and forth, rolling across communities in waves of destruction that kill thousands but accomplish little else."

By the end of 2013, around 2.3 million refugees had fled Syria, while millions more were displaced internally. An estimated 126,000 had been killed in fighting by the end of the year, up from around 93,000 in June 2013. As 2014 began, there seemed to be little likelihood of a true breakthrough that could end the conflict. In January, peace talks began in Geneva between the National Coalition and the Syrian government, but no progress was reported by the time they came to an end in February. At the same time, the United States began questioning the verifiability of death tolls in the conflict, and in February 2014 national intelligence director James Clapper warned that the conflict could become a stalemate as government forces continued bombing cities like Aleppo.

Although government forces retook Homs after multiple years of siege and fighting, few other gains were made for either the rebels or the Syrian regime. The year 2014 was largely dominated by the growth and spread of ISIS, which declared a caliphate in June. The group held territory between Aleppo and eastern Iraq at that point and carried out attacks against air force bases, Kurdish communities, and villages over the course of the year. In August 2014, ISIS took control of the city of Raqqa, which they have since made their de facto capital.

The crisis deepened as 2014 went on, with an estimated seventy-six thousand killed over the course of the year. The refugee populations in Jordan, Turkey, Lebanon, and other neighboring countries increased significantly by the end of the year, and in November international groups began calling for greater support to these countries to help ease the economic burden upon them. As the year ended, the almost four-year-old conflict was a stalemate characterized by widespread displacement and suffering.

CHAPTER 4

A CONTINUED CRISIS

Accoring to the Washington Institute for Near East Policy, as of 2015 the population of Syria was becoming geographically divided by ethnic identity. The United Nations estimate of the death toll rose to 250,000 in 2015, with some estimates reaching as high as 470,000 by early 2016. If the highest estimates, including those that count injuries, are correct, 11.5 percent of Syria's entire population has been either injured or killed in fighting. Meanwhile, an additional 6.6 million people have been internally displaced, and around 5 million have fled the country for neighboring states or Europe.

THREATS OF A PROXY WAR

In September 2015, the Russian government claimed that their forces had carried out their first air strikes in Syria against ISIS. The United States and others have accused Russia of targeting rebel areas and providing support for Assad's forces. This international involvement complicates the conflict because it brings to the table tensions between the United States and Russia, as well as between the United States and Iran. The Syrian Civil War can easily become an issue between them based not on the war itself, but on outside concerns, like the Iranian nuclear program or Russian interference in Eastern Europe. Iran and Turkey are on opposing sides of the Syrian Civil War but have close diplomatic relations and strong trade ties. Similarly, US support for Kurdish fighters has caused a break with Turkey, a US ally, which has long opposed Kurdish sovereignty and engaged in combat with militias that fought ISIS with US backing.

Abu Mohammed al-Julani is the leader of al-Nusra Front. The group broke from ISIS and eventually left behind al-Qaeda.

International involvement has also kept the conflict going by bringing supplies and weapons to both sides without giving a conclusive advantage to any side. Meanwhile, the international community has mediated peace talks between the Syrian government and some rebel factions that were undermined by air strikes and aid.

International involvement has also involved ethnic cleansing. Militant groups started targeting ethnic and religious minorities early on, including the Alawite minority that is associated with the Assad government. Alawite civilians have been targeted specifically as proxies for the Assad regime. In 2015, al-Nusra Front called on its followers to attack Alawites in response to air strikes by Russia, an ally of the Assad regime.

In late 2015, the Syrian government, backed by Russia, began retaking territory from rebel groups, starting with Homs in December. In late 2016 and early 2017, government forces retook eastern Aleppo from rebels after years of bombing that portion of the city. As the country's largest city and the rebels' last urban stronghold, it marked a potential turning point in the conflict. But concerns about ethnic cleansing spread quickly as reports of government forces killing civilians surfaced. A deal was made and put into place quickly enough to ensure that civilians were allowed to leave the city safely. However, prior to gaining control of eastern Aleppo, and by some reports even as forces were entering the city, government fighters were accused of carrying out ethnic cleansing in order to exterminate those who were not loyal to Assad.

THE REFUGEE CRISIS SPREADS

In 2015, the refugee crisis began to overwhelm Europe. An estimated one million refugees entered Europe in 2015, with 35 percent coming from Syria. And this was on top of previous refugee flights from Syria. Refugee camps have been established in Turkey, Lebanon, Jordan, and Iraq, while thousands more people have made the journey to the European Union. An estimated five million people have left Syria, while over six million have become displaced within the country. The situation is considered one of the greatest humanitarian disasters of our time. The Syrian refugee situation combined with refugees from other countries has created the largest number of refugees since World War II.

In the Middle East, Syrian refugees have become part of an already critical refugee situation. In Lebanon and Jordan, where Syrians made up one in four and one in ten people in the country respectively as of March 2017, refugee camps were already crowded with people fleeing violence in Iraq, Palestine, and elsewhere. In Turkey, almost three million Syrians have registered, with twenty-three camps housing many of them near the border, where they are vulnerable to attack. Around 230,000 Syrian refugees are staying in Iraq, where the government is fighting ISIS.

The journey to Europe is long and dangerous, often involving either an unsafe trip across the Mediterranean or across Eastern Europe. An entire industry has grown around the need to smuggle people into Europe, and families often

Jordanian soldiers look out over sixteen thousand Syrian refugees who have gathered to cross into Jordan. Over a month, four thousand refugees joined the twelve thousand that arrived in December 2016.

have to spend their entire savings in order to pay for passage. But those who smuggle refugees often cut corners by sending large groups in unsafe small rafts or boats that capsize or in the backs of trucks that easily overheat. Thousands have died making the trip. For those who arrive, they find themselves limited by scarce resources and a long process for claiming asylum, while the countries they arrive in struggle to meet their needs or agree on how to best ensure their safety.

ALAN KURDI: THE BOY ON THE BEACH

For those making the journey from the Middle East to Europe, the trip is often deadly. Around 350,000 Syrians sought refuge in Europe in 2015, the highest number from any one country. Thousands died each year.

One of those who died during the journey across the Mediterranean was Alan Kurdi, a three-year-old Syrian boy. Kurdi's family fled when ISIS attacked Kobani in 2015. His family was reportedly on their way to Canada to seek asylum when they were put on a small boat in September 2015 on the coast of Turkey. Just minutes into the approximately thirty-minute journey to the Greek island of Kos, the overpacked boat capsized. The next morning, Kurdi, his mother and brother, and other victims were found on the Turkish beach they had departed from.

The Turkish border is 4.3 miles (7 kilometers) from the Greek island of Kos (*lower right*). Those who smuggle refugees to Kos often refuse to supply them with functional life jackets.

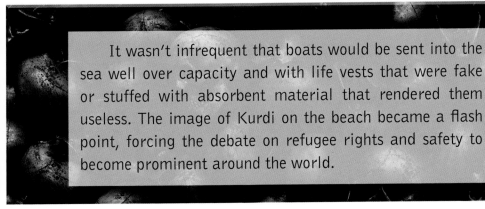

It wasn't infrequent that boats would be sent into the sea well over capacity and with life vests that were fake or stuffed with absorbent material that rendered them useless. The image of Kurdi on the beach became a flash point, forcing the debate on refugee rights and safety to become prominent around the world.

TALKS CONTINUE

The United Nations proposed the Four Committees Initiative in July 2015 to move peace talks between the opposition and the government forward, but the opposition didn't accept those terms. In May and October 2015, two rounds of peace talks among opposition groups were held in Astana, Kazakhstan. Since then, Astana has become a hub of negotiation, along with Geneva.

In October 2015, peace talks were held in Vienna that included the United Nations, the United States, Russia, and numerous others, including opposition leaders and government officials. Ceasefires were agreed upon at points throughout 2016, but all of them collapsed. Perhaps the most successful negotiation was the one that saw civilians safely out of eastern Aleppo when Syrian government forces laid siege in late 2016, but success of that sort has been rare.

In March 2017, talks in Astana between the government and opposition showed promise when all parties were able to agree to terms for a ceasefire that had yet to be implemented. Importantly, at the talks Iran joined Turkey and Russia as a guarantor state to the

On March 15, 2017, Iran, Turkey, Russia, and groups fighting in the Syrian Civil War discussed a ceasefire in Astana, Kazakhstan.

possible ceasefire, which would make Iran a responsible party in making sure any agreement is followed. Iran has had considerable relations with the Syrian regime, much as Turkey has with the rebel coalition, and could put pressure on Assad to follow through on his end of potential agreements. It marks a turning point as Turkey, Russia, and Iran take the lead in international negotiations to end the conflict, instead of Syria relying on the United States and the United Nations to initiate a satisfactory ending.

CHAPTER 5

THE FUTURE OF SYRIA

There remain many consequences of the conflict that need to be addressed in the short term. Some of them include immediate needs, like helping those most at risk of facing violence, providing aid to those who have been hurt and need sustenance, helping the millions of refugees to settle into new homes and put their lives back together, and establishing safe zones for humanitarian workers and the civilians they help. Long-term goals include ending the fighting, confronting extremist groups, and bringing lasting stability to Syria.

UNITED NATIONS PROSECUTION

It is possible for individuals to be held accountable for their role in ethnic cleansing. In December 2016, the United Nations General Assembly approved a measure establishing a panel to investigate and prosecute war crimes and crimes against humanity in Syria, known as the Mechanism (short for the International, Impartial

The International Criminal Court is the tribunal that prosecutes crimes against humanity. It is located in The Hague, in the Netherlands.

and Independent Mechanism to Assist in the Investigation and Prosecution of Those Responsible for the Most Serious Crimes under International Law Committed in Syria since March 2011). The panel will work with the Independent International Commission of Inquiry on Syria, another United Nations body, to "collect, consolidate, preserve, and analyse evidence pertaining to violations and abuses of human rights and humanitarian law," according to the United Nations.

The Mechanism's work is still in its early days, and it could take years before they are ready to bring a case before international authorities. Even when they do, there are cases in which those against whom warrants are issued are able to evade trial by simply not going to countries that would arrest them; some leaders have been able to avoid arrest for years after warrants are issued. It is unlikely that any true action could be taken until the war is brought to an end. This is in part because it is difficult to gather evidence and information that could be used to support the case at the International Criminal Court in the Netherlands. But even so, this is the first step in an important part of the healing process—holding accountable those who have committed horrible crimes.

LOOKING FORWARD

As of June 2017, it was still unclear how the Syrian Civil War would be resolved. With the international involvement that fueled fighting continuing, the long-standing ethnic and religious tensions that exist, and little will to end the war, civilians remained at risk. The conflict has claimed thousands of lives and impacted millions more, while the international community continued to work to find a solution that could bring peace and stability to the country.

Although it is unclear what the solution will look like, experts agree that overcoming the divisions that have resulted from ethnic cleansing in Syria will be key to ensuring lasting peace. And it must occur in a landscape that has seen once-diverse areas become more and more culturally and ethnically homogeneous. Reintroducing diversity to these areas would likely remind those involved of everything that went wrong and would require planning to make the transition smooth. But it would help the healing process after a long, bloody war.

A MILITARY SOLUTION

A conflict with over one thousand factions is inherently difficult to overcome. While a political solution is the international community's preferred method to end the conflict, a military solution could emerge or could reshape the dynamics at the negotiation table. As the Syrian government retakes territory from rebels, it becomes less likely that the rebels will overthrow the Assad regime using force. It is possible that the government could retake the majority of the country, forcing the rebels to accept only a partial victory as the war's end or the rebels may be completely overtaken.

In order to stop the war and ethnic cleansing in Syria, it is also important to eliminate the extremist groups fighting there. But it is not always clear who is fighting whom, and the level of violence taking place in Syria makes it nearly impossible to focus all energy on one threat. But as long as groups like ISIS and al-Nusra Front are functioning in Syria, peace cannot be achieved. There is also the question of rebuilding the country's destroyed infrastructure, resources, and cities, all of which have been decimated by the conflict and will leave citizens vulnerable even in peace.

LIFE AFTER ETHNIC CLEANSING

Syria could benefit from policies to rebuild national identity that other societies enacted after instances of genocide. Rwanda and Bosnia both experienced a period of ethnic cleansing in the 1990s and have since worked to overcome the divisions the conflicts

Battle for control in Syria

The U.S.-backed Kurdish and Syrian Arab force (SDF) has resumed its assault on Islamic State-held Tabqa dam after a temporary pause on Monday to allow engineers to inspect the dam. The U.S.-led coalition has said there is no imminent risk to the dam, unless IS intends to blow it up.

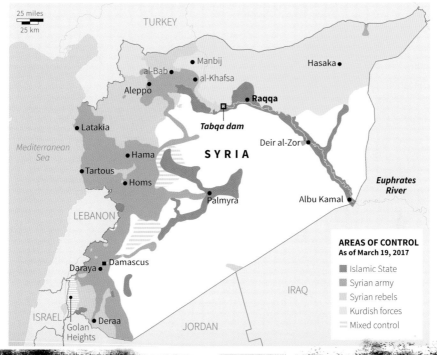

The division of territory in Syria is based on the power of each group's military might and how far it can spread while maintaining previous gains.

caused. Both countries have undertaken intensive efforts, including bringing those responsible to justice in order to hold them accountable and conducting public education campaigns that emphasize unity. After the Rwandan genocide, these efforts included bringing together victims and perpetrators of violence in neutral settings to allow them to communicate and work through the grief they both felt. And in Bosnia, the international

HOW YOU CAN HELP

There are several ways to help those in need during a conflict such as the Syrian Civil War. Organizations that provide aid to the most vulnerable people in the country and to refugees need resources. There are many ways you can get involved. Here are a few ideas:

Raise Funds Get some friends together or work with a teacher at your school to organize a fundraiser. Then, donate the proceeds to an organization like UNICEF or Save the Children. Both of those groups are working to help children in Syria get the care, food, and education they need.

Make Your Voice Heard Let your leaders know how you feel by writing letters telling them that you care about peace in Syria. You can find information about your local representatives at house.gov, along with how to send them letters. You can also write letters to refugees to let them know you hope they are safe. Learn more about how to do that at CARE.org.

Educate Yourself One of the best things we can do to help Syria is stay aware of what is happening there. There's a lot of information and news out there, but you can ask your parents or teacher to help you stay up to date on the latest developments in peace talks. You can also talk with your friends and let them know what's going on in Syria—and brainstorm more ways to help!

community helped assure those displaced by conflict the safe right of return, or the right to come back to the area from which they had fled. These conciliatory actions helped to integrate persecuted groups back into society at large and paved the way for institutional changes to prevent another genocide.

This photo shows a street in Aleppo. Like many other cities and villages in Syria, it was left in ruins. This particular city was destroyed when Assad's forces retook it from rebels in January 2017.

Issues that still exist in Syria include that refugees living in camps in the Middle East or in centers in Europe have no viable way to safely return to their country or resume their lives. The economy and infrastructure need to be rebuilt, and the millions who could potentially come back to the country will need access to resources. But before any of these reforms can happen, the war must end.

TIMELINE

1916 The Sykes-Picot Agreement carves out the modern country of Syria.

1920 Syria comes under French control and is divided into three regions, including one for Alawites and one for the Druze.

1936 Syrians protest French rule and convince the French to negotiate a treaty of Syrian independence. France, however, would never ratify that treaty.

1946 The last French troops finally leave Syria.

1970 Hafez al-Assad seizes power in a military coup and declares himself president.

2000 Bashar al-Assad, Hafez's son, succeeds him as president in an uncontested election.

2011 Protests known as the Arab Spring sweep across the Middle East and North Africa. Syria becomes involved in protests on March 6.

The Assad regime responds to widespread protests with violence on March 18.

The Arab League begins the first talk to end the Syrian Civil War in November.

2012 The first ceasefire is agreed upon, but it collapses shortly after being implemented.

2013 The United Nations concludes that Syrian government forces have used chemical weapons against civilians in a suburb of Damascus.

2014 ISIS declares a caliphate in territory across Syria and Iraq and chooses Raqqa for its capital.

2015 On September 30, Russia begins air strikes against ISIS, but Western governments believe Russians target rebels as well.

Talks begin in Astana among opposition groups on October 2.

2016 On December 22, government forces retake Aleppo.

On the same day, the United Nations establishes a panel to investigate and prosecute war crimes in Syria.

2017 Peace talks resume in Astana and Geneva.

GLOSSARY

Alawite A minority faith in Syria that blends Shia Islam and other Abrahamic faiths. The Assad family, which rules Syria, is Alawite, which has meant that the government and military is largely Alawite as well.

Arab League An organization that fosters cooperation between Arabic-speaking countries.

Arab Spring Popular protests that took place across the Middle East and North Africa in 2011.

authoritarian Having to do with a government that allows few personal freedoms or guaranteed human rights to its subjects.

caliphate An Islamic empire that controlled the Middle East, North Africa, and parts of Spain at various times between the seventh century and the twentieth century.

Druze A small religious and ethnic minority living in Syria whose beliefs blend teachings from Islam and Christianity.

ethnic cleansing Targeted policies of violence and/or displacement that remove an entire ethnic group from an area.

extremist Intolerant political or religious beliefs far outside of the mainstream.

genocide The deliberate and planned killing of a large population of a specific trait like ethnicity, race, or religion.

Gulf Emirates The states along the Arab Gulf, including Qatar and Bahrain.

homogeneous Being uniform in race, ethnicity, religion, belief, or other manner of being.

humanitarian crisis A conflict or natural disaster that threatens the safety and health of a large group of people.

Kurds The world's largest stateless ethnic group that mostly consists of people living in Turkey, Iran, Iraq, and Syria.

mandate An authority to govern an area that the League of Nations provides.

per capita GDP The economic output of a country divided by the population. This doesn't account for unequal wealth within the population.

proxies In warfare, when two rivals fight indirectly by supporting opposing sides of a conflict.

sectarianism Divisions along religious lines that often enable conflict or tension.

self-immolation Setting oneself on fire as protest.

Shia A sect of Islam that believes the prophet Muhammad designated his successor to be Ali ibn Abi Talib.

stateless A person or group of people who are not recognized as citizens of any country.

Sunni A sect of Islam that believes that the prophet Muhammad did not designate a successor, which is why Abu Bakr (the prophet's father-in-law) was elected to be the first successor. They are considered to be orthodox believers.

Sykes-Picot Agreement A 1916 agreement between France and Great Britain that drew the modern boundaries of the Middle East and established French and British control of the region.

Syrian Ba'ath Party The governing party in Syria that the Assad family heads.

Yazidis An ancient religious minority of ethnic Kurds in Iraq.

Amnesty International
600 Pennsylvania Avenue SE
Washington, DC 20003
(202) 544-0200
Website: http://www.amnestyusa.org
Facebook: @amnestyusa
Twitter: @amnesty
Instagram: @amnesty
This international group monitors and documents human rights
abuses, including ethnic cleansing, and advocates for human
rights protections.

Canadian Council for Refugees
6839 Drolet #301
Montréal, QC H2S 2T1
Canada
(514) 277-7223
Website: http://ccrweb.ca
Facebook: @ccrweb
Twitter: @ccrweb
This council advocates for refugees and migrants in Canada. They
encourage Canada's resettlement program and work to protect
various internationally exploited populations.

International Rescue Committee
122 East 42nd Street, #12
New York, NY 10168
(212) 551-3000
Website: https://www.rescue.org
Facebook: @InternationalRescueCommittee
Twitter: @TheIRC

Instagram: @TheIRC
This rapid-response group tracks the humanitarian impact
of conflicts to offer health, safety, education, and economic aid to
those impacted by humanitarian crises.

Lifeline Syria
40 University Avenue, Suite 420
Toronto, ON M5J 1T1
Canada
(647) 943-6300
http://lifelinesyria.ca
Facebook: @lifelinesyria
Twitter: @LifelineSyria
This organization helps to sponsor the permanent resettlement of
Syrian refugees in Toronto.

Save the Children
899 North Capitol Street NE, #900
Washington, DC 20002
(202) 640-6600
Website: http://www.savethechildren.org
Facebook: @SavetheChildren
Twitter: @SavetheChildren
Instagram: @SavetheChildren
This international organization advocates for children by
organizing sponsorships and volunteers and raising funds for
impoverished children, including refugees and those living in
war zones.

United Nations
820 2nd Avenue, 15th Floor
New York, NY 10017
(212) 661-1313
Website: https://www.un.int/syria

Facebook: @unitednations
Twitter: @un
Instagram: @unitednations
This international organization conducts peace talks and efforts to end war. They share human rights reports and agreements passed by the United Nations Security Council.

WEBSITES

Because of the changing nature of internet links, Rosen Publishing has developed an online list of websites related to the subject of this book. This site is updated regularly. Please use this link to access this list:

http://www.rosenlinks.com/BWGE/Syrian

FOR FURTHER READING

Cunningham, Anne. *Critical Perspectives on Immigrants and Refugees*. New York, NY: Enslow Publishing, 2016.

Danaher, Paul. *The New Middle East: The World After the Arab Spring*. London, UK: Bloomsbury, 2015.

Habeeb, William Mark. *The Middle East in Turmoil: Conflict, Revolution, and Change*. Santa Barbara, CA: Greenwood Publishing, 2012.

Heing, Bridey. *Geography, Government, and Conflict Across the Middle East*. New York, NY: Cavendish Square Publishing, 2017.

Marsico, Katie. *ISIS*. New York, NY: ABDO Publishing, 2015.

Maxim, Bailey, ed. *The Colonial and Postcolonial Middle East*. New York, NY: Britannica Educational Publishing, 2017

McHugo, John. *Syria: A Recent History*. London: Saqi Books, 2015.

McNabb, Brian. *A Military History of the Modern Middle East*. New York, NY: Gale, 2017.

Sorenson, David S. *Syria in Ruins: The Dynamics of the Syrian Civil War*. Santa Barbara, CA: Praeger, 2017.

Sullivan, Anne Marie. *Syria*. New York, NY: Mason Crest, 2015.

BIBLIOGRAPHY

Abboud, Samer N. *Syria*. New York, NY: Polity Press, 2015.

Balanche, Fabrice. "Ethnic Cleansing Threatens Syria's Unity." The Washington Institute, December 3, 2015. http://www .washingtoninstitute.org/policy-analysis/view/ethnic-cleansing -threatens-syrias-unity.

Bar, Karim el-. "'Ethnic Cleansing on an Unprecedented Scale': Rebels, UN Criticise Assad Tactics." Middle East Eye, September 3, 2016. http://www.middleeasteye.net/news /ethnic-cleansing-unprecedented-scale-rebels-un-criticize -assad-tactics-954614280.

BBC News. "Migrant crisis: Migration to Europe Explained in Seven Charts." March 4, 2016. http://www.bbc.co.uk/news/world -europe-34131911.

Dooley, Brian. "Ending Sectarianism in Syria." *Foreign Affairs*, April 13, 2016. https://www.foreignaffairs.com/articles/syria/2016-04-13 /ending-sectarianism-syria.

Erlich, Reese. *Inside Syria: The Backstory of Their Civil War and What the World Can Expect*. Amherst, NY: Prometheus Books, 2014.

Escritt, Thomas. "Syrian, Russian Forces Carrying Out Ethnic Cleansing Around Aleppo: Turkish PM." Reuters, February 10, 2016. http://www.reuters.com/article/us-mideast-crisis-syria-turkey -davutoglu-idUSKCN0VJ1MK.

Fromkin, David. *A Peace to End All Peace: The Fall of the Ottoman Empire and the Creation of the Modern Middle East*. New York, NY: Henry Holt and Co., 1989.

Gerges, Fawaz A. *ISIS: A History*. Princeton, NJ: Princeton University Press, 2016.

Human Rights Watch. "Syria." Retrieved February 22, 2017. https:// www.hrw.org/middle-east/n-africa/syria.

Laub, Zachary. "Who's Who in Syria's Civil War." Council on Foreign Relations, December 22, 2016. http://www.cfr.org/syria/s-syrias-civil-war/p38607.

Mercy Corps. "Quick Facts: What You Need to Know About the Syria Crisis." October 13, 2016. https://www.mercycorps.org/articles/iraq-jordan-lebanon-syria-turkey/quick-facts-what-you-need-know-about-syria-crisis.

Ottaway, Marina. "Does the Middle East Need New Borders?" Foreign Affairs, April 14, 2016. https://www.foreignaffairs.com/articles/middle-east/2016-04-14/does-middle-east-need-new-borders.

Stavridis, James. "Syrian Ghosts." Foreign Policy, November 6, 2015. http://foreignpolicy.com/2015/11/06/lessons-from-the-balkans-for-syria.

United Nations News Centre. "Syria: UN Approves Mechanism to Lay Groundwork for Investigations Into Possible War Crimes." December 22, 2016. http://www.un.org/apps/news/story.asp?NewsID=55862#.WK4NyjsrKM9.

Worth, Robert F. *A Rage for Order: The Middle East in Turmoil, from Tahrir Square to ISIS*. New York, NY: Farrar, Strauss and Giroux, 2016.

INDEX

ABOUT THE AUTHOR

Bridey Heing is a writer and book critic based in Washington, DC. She holds degrees in political science and international affairs from DePaul University and Washington University in Saint Louis. Her areas of focus are comparative politics and Iranian politics. Her masters' thesis explores the evolution of populist politics and democracy in Iran since 1900. She has written about Iranian affairs, women's rights, art, and politics for publications like *The Economist*, *Hyperallergic*, and *The Establishment*. She also writes about literature and film. She enjoys traveling, reading, and exploring the many museums of Washington, DC.

PHOTO CREDITS

Cover (inset), pp. 19, 29, 44 Anadolu Agency/Getty Images; cover (cracked texture) Marbury/Shutterstock.com; pp. 4, 42 © iStockphoto .com/PeterHermesFurian; p. 8 Kaveh Kazemi/Getty Images; pp. 10, 38 © AP Images; p. 12 AWAD AWAD/AFP/Getty Images; p. 17 Fethi Belaid/AFP/Getty Images; p. 21 Rami Al-Sayed/AFP/Getty Images; p. 23 Kyodo News/Getty Images; p. 27 Anwar Amro/AFP/Gety Images; p. 32 John Moore/Getty Images; p. 34 AFP/Getty Images; p. 41 Khalil Mazraawi/AFP/Getty Images; p. 46 Michel Porro/Getty Images; p. 49 Jessica Wang/RTR/Newscom; p. 51 Louai Beshara/AFP/Getty Images; pp. 9, 22, 33, 42, 43 (top), 50 rangizzz/Shutterstock.com.

Design: Brian Garvey; Layout: Erica Vermeulen;
Editor: Bernadette Davis; Photo Research: Karen Huang